Martingale®
& C O M P A N Y

Everyday STYLE

CLASSIC KNITS FOR WOMEN

SSEN NOBLE

Everyday Style: Classic Knits for Women
© 2006 by Carol Rasmussen Noble

Martingale & Company
20205 144th Avenue NE
Woodinville, WA 98072-8478 USA
www.martingale-pub.com

President .... NANCY J. MARTIN
CEO .... DANIEL J. MARTIN
VP and General Manager .... TOM WIERZBICKI
Publisher .... JANE HAMADA
Editorial Director .... MARY V. GREEN
Managing Editor .... TINA COOK
Technical Editor .... KAREN COSTELLO SOLTYS
Copy Editor .... LIZ MCGEHEE
Design Director .... STAN GREEN
Illustrators .... ROBIN STROBEL AND LAUREL STRAND
Cover and Text Designer .... STAN GREEN
Studio Photographer .... BRENT KANE
Fashion Photographer .... J. P. HAMEL
Fashion Stylist .... PAM SIMPSON
Hair and Makeup Stylist .... LORI SMITH

DEDICATION

To my father

ACKNOWLEDGMENTS

I wish to thank the entire staff of Martingale & Company for their encouragement, help, and professionalism. They make beautiful books. My husband and family have been extremely supportive, as have Margaret F. Dalrymple, Claudia Judson Chesney, Galina Alexandrovna Khmeleva, and Margaret Leask Peterson of Shetland. Heartfelt thanks to all.

Contents

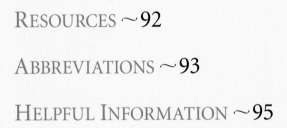

Introduction

Have you ever had a favorite thing you loved to wear? Perhaps a soft, old cardigan—first thing to put on in the morning and last to take off at night. Or something oversized and comfortable for winter days at home. Is it a lace shawl or an evening sweater that makes you look and feel especially attractive? Something crisp for the office, or perhaps fuzzy angora with a pretty ribbon closure—all in your favorite colors of course. My personal answer is a definite "Yes!" With this focus in mind, I have designed this collection with variety, style, and comfort so that every prospective knitter may find her particular favorite among its patterns.

Most of us have very busy lives. Nevertheless, more and more of us are picking up knitting needles for both relaxation and a desire for self-expression. And, perhaps most importantly, because there is a deep, quiet joy in making something beautiful with the skill of our own hands. On a practical level, we all want to knit something that fits well and reflects our personal style, whether we have entry-level skills or we have advanced further. Given well-designed patterns, we can personalize our clothing to make a statement about ourselves that doesn't just come off a rack.

As a designer, it's my goal to help you make such a statement, by pulling together shape, color, yarn, and stitch patterns into an overall blend that becomes more than just the sum of its parts. My job is to be an interpreter—I listen to yarns as I listen to people; the yarns tell me what they want to be. The end result is a coherent, successful design for a cherished garment. And the good news is that such patterns don't have to be at all difficult to knit. I believe in simplicity of design and technique. I'm not one who relishes the overly complicated.

Rather, I prefer to design user-friendly patterns that are accessible by a very wide audience of all experience levels.

If you ask me what I think looks best on most women, I will say without hesitation: classic lines. This doesn't mean plain, or boxy, or uninteresting, or even terribly traditional. Rather, it means that the sweater or shawl in question will have an understated elegance, whether it's for a weekend outdoors or a brilliantly lit evening. Detail doesn't have to be fussy, and color doesn't have to be overwhelming or dull. The fit should be flattering whether you're large or petite. The design techniques I developed for *Style at Large* (Martingale & Company, 2003) will thin a large woman as well as a smaller woman. You'll find those same techniques used in this book, in patterns designed and written for all sizes.

The emphasis in this collection is on making a sweater or shawl that looks beautiful and complicated but that is actually simple to knit. Beginners need not look elsewhere. Many of the pieces involve only knit-and-purl patterning. These stitches are in everyone's repertoire, and

they offer so many interesting effects. Add to those basics the two most common decreases and yarn overs, and you have the basic stitches needed to knit a totally wonderful wardrobe. Your garments will have a "designer" feel that belies their simplicity—and all without stranding colors or picking up a cable needle!

I have used standard yarn weights throughout, and I discuss yarn substitutions in the introduction to each pattern. My patterns provide accessibility for the knitter who wants to make the design exactly as it appears in the book; at the same time, I encourage you to use the patterns as a jumping-off point to fashion your own favorite sweaters and shawls. With a few minor exceptions, I have used all-natural fibers in hand paints, heathers, and solids. And don't worry if you live in a warm climate—many wools and cottons can be interchanged with excellent results.

In this collection I have tried to design something for everyone. My garments are neither cute, nor ethnic, nor faddish. They are easy classics whose beauty, style, and wearability will remain fresh year after year. I hope you will find your favorite here!

—*Carol Rasmussen Noble*

Knitting Tips and Techniques

In this section you'll find techniques that work especially well for me. I urge you to read this section before starting any of the designs in the book and refer back to it during knitting, since I used these techniques in the designs. My hope is that you'll find this advice useful and that you'll be able to incorporate a new tip or two into your own knitting.

TOOLS OF THE TRADE

You'll find lots of needles and notions available for knitting, and often the tools you choose to use are simply based on personal preferences. Here are some of my guidelines for selecting tools; perhaps they'll work for you too.

The best needles for you. I feel that straight needles are best in almost all cases for knitting back and forth. Although some knitters prefer circular needles, I find that with their different diameters at needle ends and cable or cord, they simply don't hold the tension evenly enough for me. It may seem more convenient to use them, but you will get a tighter, smoother, more even surface with straight needles. In particular, I find 16" and 11" circular needles to be especially hard to work with, so I almost always use double-pointed needles in place of them. Once you master the double-pointed technique, the knitting progresses just as rapidly.

If you've experienced pain while knitting, try knitting on different projects for shorter periods of time. It also helps to knit on smaller, shorter needles with finer yarn. Also, try quieting your hand and wrist movement and loosening your grip. That said, use the tools that work best for you, and please keep on knitting.

You'll find a wide variety of needles to choose from, so use these pointers to help you narrow down the choices. If you tend to knit tightly, use metal needles because the yarn will slip easily; if you tend to knit loosely, use bamboo needles because the yarn will cling more to bamboo. Exotic wood and plastic needles fall somewhere in between. Remember that bamboo and plastic needles are flexible, and wood needles will break if stressed.

I find flexibility to be very important in a needle because it allows the needle rather than my joints to take the stress of movement. Also watch out for exotic woods—they are pretty, but they splinter. And when I knit lace, such as the Highland Mist shawl on page 37, tension is very important, so I use needles no longer than 10".

They give the best control over my stitches and the piece as a whole.

Tips on choosing yarns. When I select yarns, I try to match the characteristics of the yarn—twist, stretch, loft, strength, and surface—to whatever pattern I'm knitting. I could go on about this forever, having learned mostly from my own mistakes. But you have to learn from your own experiences what works for you. Nothing is worse than investing time, money, and commitment in a project that doesn't turn out the way you would like. Seek advice if you're unsure, but don't ignore your intuition. In this book I have tried to suggest suitable yarn alternatives for all of the garments so that if you prefer one type of fiber over another, you'll know what to look for to obtain the best results.

The importance of gauge. Gauge is extremely important to the fit of your finished garment. It's also highly individualistic; needle size is less relevant. Make sure that you do adequate gauge swatches before starting a project. Don't worry about what size needles the yarn label or directions call for—use what works for you.

The classic way to determine your gauge is to knit a 20-stitch by 20-row piece. Then measure the width of the swatch and divide the number of stitches by the number of inches to get the stitches per inch. For example, if 20 stitches measures 4", 20 divided by 4 equals 5 stitches per inch. Repeat the process with rows and the length of the piece. If your gauge isn't as specified in the pattern, you should change your needle size. For a pattern stitch, knit a swatch containing two or three horizontal and vertical pattern repeats, count the stitches and rows, and do the arithmetic in the same manner as above.

Don't forget markers. When working cables or lace patterns, stitch markers are extremely helpful. Place them between cable sections or lace repeats. That way, your counting is simplified and it's much easier to catch mistakes early, especially such things as dropped yarn overs.

Markers help you visualize. There are many types of markers on the market. I prefer rubber markers because they grip the needle. You can even make your own marker out of a short length of smooth, contrasting yarn tied with a slipknot.

FAVORITE TECHNIQUES

In knitting patterns and books you will often find conflicting advice on how to do things. The following are my own tried-and-true techniques. I encourage you to try them.

Knots for durability. I'm not a knitter who abhors knots. I like my knitting to be durable enough to hold together through heavy use and repeated washings, so I always tie on threads, even in lace. But don't use square knots, which are notorious for slipping apart. I always use a overhand knot. I've found that if you weave in your ends with the proper amount of tension, neither the doubling nor the knot will show on the surface, so you don't always need to end your yarn at the beginning or end of a row if you're running short of yarn.

Overhand knot

The Noble neck. I hate loose, sloppy necks, so I devised a neck based on ratios instead of on the number of stitches. No matter what size you're knitting or yarn weight you're using, and regardless of the neck width or depth, the ratio will produce a perfect neck every time.

An unfinished neck has four basic areas—the front bind off, the back bind off, and the two diagonal edges (which may be slightly curved) that connect the bind offs. I pick up one out of every two stitches on the diagonals, two out of every three stitches on the front bind off, and three out of every four stitches on the back bind off. The actual number of stitches picked up is immaterial, except when you need to balance a pattern repeat.

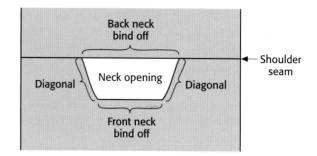

If you do need to balance a repeat of a certain number of stitches, you may need to pick up or drop extra stitches. I always make this accommodation at the left shoulder seam, although you can also use the right shoulder seam if necessary. First, I do the pickup and then make any needed adjustment on the first row by either knitting two stitches together or increasing a stitch. In making the adjustment, I usually add stitches rather than decrease stitches because it fills out the edge. This way, no additional holes are made. Consult a basic knitting reference for making standard increases and decreases.

A problem that plagues sweater necks is the appearance of holes along the join with the body. It's very easy to avoid this problem, however, if you twist each of your picked-up stitches as you work the first row by knitting into the back of them as shown below. This method will produce a smooth, tight join. It's also good for picking up stitches on the front bands of a cardigan, for fingers or thumbs in gloves and mittens, for picking up sleeve-edge stitches in Fair Isle knitting, or for picking up slipped stitches on a lace edge. The basic idea is to close the gap by producing a herringbone. Also, when working necks (or anything) in the round on double-pointed needles, make sure to pull up the yarn extra tightly at the needle change to avoid a line of loose stitches or holes.

Knit into the back of the stitch.

Holding stitches. You will notice that some patterns call for putting the shoulder stitches on a spare needle instead of on a stitch holder. This is only done with shoulders that are to be joined with a three-needle bind off, which requires that the spare stitches be on needles to work the seam. For other, smaller areas, stitch holders can certainly be used. My personal preference, however, is to use a crochet hook to put the spare stitches on a loop of smooth, tightly twisted waste yarn and tie it off in a loop. Holders are awkward to knit around, and many times using them requires extra steps to get the stitch transferred back onto the needles so they are facing in the correct direction for the bind off.

I also highly recommend binding off front neck and back neck stitches, rather than putting them on any sort of holder. This gives a stable, nonstretchy edge that will keep the neck fitting as it's supposed to through much wear and washing.

Front bands. My preferred method for doing front bands is to pick up stitches on the vertical edge and then knit them outward. I pick up three out of every four stitches on the edge and twist each of them on the first row as described for necks, opposite. The only difference is that if you need to make an adjustment in the number of stitches, you should space the increases or decreases evenly along the body of the band, not at either end. Remember that buttonholes go on the right front band for women and on the left front band for men. Also, always bind off loosely in pattern to avoid distorting the band.

Easy buttonholes. My recommended buttonhole is simple. It does not involve binding off and casting on, it leaves no gaps or loops, and it accommodates every size button and thickness of yarn. It's a four-stitch round buttonhole done over two rows.

- When you get to within two stitches of your buttonhole placement on the right side of the piece, knit two together, double yarn over, knit two together. Continue in pattern.

- On the reverse row for these four stitches: work one stitch in pattern, purl into first loop of double yarn over, knit into second loop of double yarn over, work one stitch in pattern.

- When you come to these four stitches on the next right-side row, work them in pattern.

Work the buttonholes on the middle two rows of your front band. (You will need an even number of rows on your front band.) The top and bottom buttonholes should be placed ½" from the top and bottom edges. Button spacing should be no closer than 2" and no farther apart than 3", unless you're trying for a special effect.

If you knit the neckband of a cardigan first and then knit the front bands along the total length, it's easy to plan your buttonholes. I always draw a simple schematic diagram and use a calculator to figure out how to evenly space whatever number of buttons I have to work with.

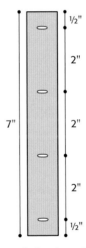

Buttonhole schematic

Buttons. When sewing buttons on the band opposite the buttonhole band, place them closer to the sweater edge than to the outside edge of the band. This way, you will create a balanced closure.

Ease and fit. Ease refers to the difference between your body measurements and the finished measurements of the garment in question. It usually refers to the bust measurement on sweaters. Without ease—in other words, without extra inches built into the design—the garment would be skintight and impossible to move in. The usual minimum ease allowance for a close-fitting sweater is 2", making the garment 2" bigger around than your bust measurement. Don't confuse this with stretch, which is *not* figured into the finished measurements. Most of the sweaters in this book have 2" to 6" of ease built into the design, which puts them into a nice medium-to-close-fit range and is in tune with today's more fitted clothing.

You'll notice in the project directions in this book that I've included two sets of bust measurements: one for the finished size of the garment and one for the size bust the garment is to fit. By subtracting the "to fit" size from the "finished" size, you'll determine the amount of wearing ease built into the pattern. If you'd like more ease (i.e., a looser garment), you can always knit a larger size to get 8" or more of ease. To figure the ease of a particular design for a particular size, subtract your bust size from the finished bust size. Also note that sweaters such as cardigans or vests that are made to be worn over other garments will have more wearing ease than those that are worn next to the body, such as a tank top or fitted T-shirt.

A final note about the sizing is that some of the sweaters have directions for three, four, or even more sizes. But a few are given in only two sizes, and that's because of the pattern stitch repeat. For some of the designs, the repeat is 15 or more stitches, and therefore it's just not possible to fit the design into a smaller number of stitches, which you would need to do for a smaller size.

Three-needle bind off (3-needle BO). Another technique I like is the three-needle bind off for joining front and back shoulders. I hate shoulders that stretch all out of shape, so I never graft them, and in my own personal knitting I never sew them. A three-needle bind off gives stability to the join and keeps the shoulders and neck where they should be when you wear

the sweater. If you do the three-needle bind off with right sides together, you will create a seam ridge on the inside of the sweater. If you do the three-needle bind off with wrong sides together, the seam ridge will be on the outside of the sweater—my personal preference. I like to use it as a design feature. For example, you can introduce a second color as the binding yarn. Just keep in mind that the front and back of the three-needle-bind-off seam look different, so make sure you bind off in the same direction on both shoulders. Binding off from the front or the back is your choice. Use the same size or smaller needles that you used to knit the sweater to hold the stitches, and a smaller needle for the working needle.

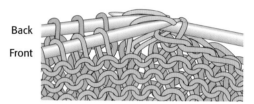

Back
Front

Right sides together, knit together 1 stitch from front needle and 1 stitch from back needle.

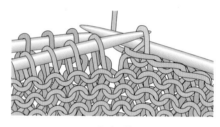

Bind off.

Washing and blocking. Every yarn works up differently. If you're not sure how the piece can best be finished or fulled, work some swatches and try different methods on them to see the results. I give washing and blocking instructions for each piece in this book. Most yarns respond well to a little blocking, even if it's just a light steaming. Steaming works very well for evening out the surface of color work. That said, never steam ribbings or textured patterns because it will flatten and stretch them.

My preferred washing method is to use lukewarm water for both the bath and the rinse. Baby shampoo is gentler than detergents, which often cause colors to run or delicate fibers to harden. I always let a sweater soak for at least an hour or two, typically overnight. That way, it literally cleans itself and doesn't require scrubbing, which can felt the yarn. On the other hand, if you're knitting with yarn that has large unspun areas—such as chunky, thick and thins, or Lopi—you'll want to felt the yarn at least a little to make the garment more durable. Some yarns can be put through the spin cycle of your washer so that they are drier for blocking and won't droop with the weight of the water. Others must be rolled in towels to remove excess moisture. When in doubt, do the latter.

Some knitting—particularly pieces that need to be pulled, stretched, and pinned to shape—must be blocked soaking wet. Do this before sewing the pieces together. If you need extra moisture, you can use a spray bottle to wet the surface. I don't have any special blocking forms; I just lay out or pin out the pieces on the carpet faceup, using T-pins. To keep pets and children away, cover the blocked piece with a towel, or place it in a room where the door can be shut, so the garment can remain undisturbed until dry.

Hand-painted yarns. Hand-painted yarns are beautiful to work with and to wear. But the colors in hand-painted yarns commonly run. Test a piece of yarn or a small swatch before leaving a sweater to soak, especially if it's variegated. In many cases, the excess dye comes out after a few washings. And, if you notice that dye is rubbing off onto your hands or needles as you knit, you can soak the piece itself and any unused skeins in a bath of white vinegar and lukewarm water to set the dye. Leave them very slightly stretched to dry.

A final word on using hand-painted yarns: Each dye lot—indeed, each skein—will be slightly different. Don't be put off by this. Simply allow the variations to enrich the color palette of your garment. Alternating between two skeins as you knit can help diminish the variances and make them virtually unnoticeable in the finished garment.

So those are my tips and techniques. I hope you've learned a few things that you can use to improve your projects. But ultimately, the craft of knitting is highly individual, and you should follow your own inclinations. Happy knitting!

Pleated Shirt

I wanted to design a sweater for heavy, worsted-weight yarn that wouldn't look or feel bulky. I also wanted to experiment with two different heather yarns used in the same sweater for an added bit of contrast. I chose a blue-and-black Shetland wool heather for the body and a blue-and-brown heather of the same yarn for the collar and cuffs. This dark color scheme, combined with shirt-style collar and cuffs and a pleated body, gives a look of understated sophistication and detailing that is formal enough for the office but comfortable enough for leisure wear. This fitted sweater is a bit dressier than a standard pullover, reminding me of a dress shirt.

But don't let the detailing fool you. The only stitches used for this sweater are knit and purl. The pleated effect comes from a rib variation, which also makes the sweater self-shaping. Those design details make it a slimming sweater that will make any woman feel well dressed and comfortable.

If Shetland wool is too warm for your climate, you can make this sweater in a luxury fiber or a blend with silk or cashmere. But make sure that whatever yarn you use has a good twist to keep it from expanding unnecessarily.

SIZE DETAILS

To Fit Bust Size: 34 (38, 42, 46)"
Finished Bust: 36 (40, 44, 48)"
Finished Length: 24 (24½, 25, 25½)"
Finished Sleeve Length: 18 (19, 20, 20)"

MATERIALS

MC—9 (10, 11, 12) skeins of Jamieson's Shetland Heather Aran (formerly Soft Shetland) from Unicorn Books and Crafts Inc. (100% wool; 101 yds/50 g skein) in color 1340 Midnight **(4)**

CC—1 (1, 1, 2) skeins of Jamieson's Shetland Heather Aran (100% wool; 101 yds/50 g skein) from Unicorn Books and Crafts Inc. in color 1180 Rosewood **(4)**

1 pair of US size 8 (5 mm) needles or size to obtain gauge

1 set of US size 8 (5 mm) double-pointed needles or size 8, 16" circular needle

Spare needles or stitch holders

2 buttons, ½"diameter, for cuffs

GAUGE

4 sts = 1"; 4 rows = 1" in body patt

SEED STITCH

(2-st, 2-row rep)

Row 1 (RS): *K1, P1; rep from * to end of row.

Row 2 (WS): *P1, K1; rep from * to end of row.

MAIN BODY PATTERN

(8-st, 16-row rep)

Row 1 (RS): *P7, K1; rep from * to end of row.

Row 2 (WS): *P2, K6; rep from * to end of row.

Row 3: *P5, K3; rep from * to end of row.

Row 4: *P4, K4; rep from * to end of row.

Row 5: *P3, K5, rep from * to end of row.

Row 6: *P6, K2; rep from * to end of row.

Row 7: *P1, K7; rep from * to end of row.

Row 8: Purl.

Row 9: *P1, K7; rep from * to end of row.

Row 10: *P6, K2; rep from * to end of row.

Row 11: *P3, K5; rep from * to end of row.

Row 12: *P4, K4; rep from * to end of row.

Row 13: *P5, K3; rep from * to end of row.

Row 14: *P2, K6; rep from * to end of row.

Row 15: *P7, K1; rep from * to end of row.

Row 16: Knit.

Rep these 16 rows for patt. If you prefer to follow a chart, see patt chart on page 19.

BACK

- CO 72 (80, 88, 96) sts. Work 3 rows of seed st.

- On next row (WS), knit across.

- On next row (RS), begin main body patt with row 1. Cont in patt until piece measures 16 (16, 16, 16½)".

- BO 8 sts at beg of next 2 rows (16 sts dec); work remainder of sts in patt.

- Cont in patt until armhole measures 7½ (8, 8½, 8½)".

- On next RS row, switch to seed st. AT SAME TIME, work 14 (16, 20, 22) sts; attach 2nd ball of yarn and BO 28 (32, 32, 36) sts; work 14 (16, 20, 22) sts. Cont in seed st until armhole measures 8 (8½, 9, 9)". Put shoulder sts on spare needle or st holder.

FRONT

- Work as for back until armhole measures 5 (5½, 6, 6)".

- On next RS row, work in patt 16 (18, 22, 24) sts; attach 2nd ball of yarn and BO 24 (28, 28, 32) sts; work rem 16 (18, 22, 24) sts in patt.

- On next RS row and following RS row, dec 1 st at each neck edge (total 4 sts dec).

- Work even until armhole measures 7½ (8, 8½, 8½)".

- On next RS row, switch to seed st and work even until armhole measures 8 (8½, 9, 9)". Put shoulder sts on spare needle or st holder.

SLEEVES *(Make 2)*

- CO 36 sts for all sizes. Work 2 rows of seed st.

- On next RS row, beg main body patt starting with st 7 in row 1 of chart. AT SAME TIME, on 5th and every subsequent 4th row (RS), inc 1 st at each edge 14 (16, 18, 18) times, keeping continuity of patt: total sts 64 (68, 72, 72).

- Cont in patt until sleeve measures 17½ (18½, 19½, 19½)".

- On next RS row, switch to seed st and work even until sleeve measures 18 (19, 20, 20)". BO all sts.

FINISHING

- Using CC, join front and back shoulder sts, using 3-needle BO (see page 12).

- With dpns and MC, starting at center front, PU 1 of every 2 sts on diagonals, 2 of every 3 sts on front neck BO, and 3 of every 4 sts on back neck BO. You'll need an even number of sts, so adjust if necessary.

- **Collar:** With left needle at center front and using CC, PU 2 sts behind and below first 2 sts on right-hand needle. Start knitting on left-hand needle. (This is right center edge of collar.) Even though you're using dpns, you will be knitting back and forth in seed st, not in the round. At end of row, on right center needle, PU 2 sts in front of and below 3rd and 4th sts on left needle (this is at left center edge of collar). Turn. Cont working back and forth in seed st until collar measures 4". BO loosely.

- Sew in sleeve tops. Sew underarm and side seams.

BIND OFF ON THE OUTSIDE

I like to do the three-needle bind off on the outside of a garment for two reasons. First, it makes the bind-off ridge on the outside, leaving the inside of the sweater smooth along the shoulder. Second, it gives me a chance to make a design statement. For this sweater, I used the brown yarn for the cuffs and collar to do the shoulder bind off, making a fine line of contrast color at the shoulder seam. Of course, you can do the bind off on the inside of the garment if you prefer, but I highly recommend that you try this technique!

- **Cuffs:** Starting at seam, PU 9 sts on each of 4 dpn. Again, you will be knitting back and forth. Then attach CC yarn between 2nd and 3rd needles on outside edge of sleeve. This is location of cuff opening. Work in seed st for 2". Then, on next RS row, inc 1 st at each cuff edge on next and following RS rows 6 times. BO all sts and fold up cuff. Overlap cuff tips and sew on button to anchor them.

- This garment does not require blocking before wear, although washing will soften yarn. To wash, soak sweater overnight in cold water and baby shampoo. In morning, rinse sweater and put it in washer on spin cycle. Lay it out flat to dry.

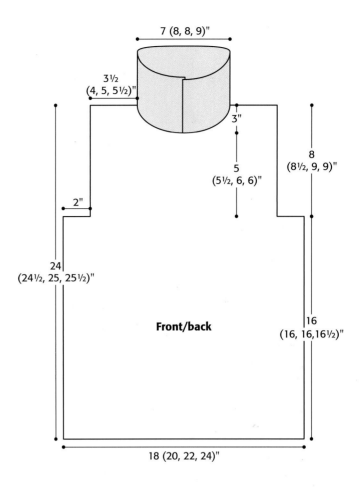

7 (8, 8, 9)"

3½
(4, 5, 5½)"

3"

5
(5½, 6, 6)"

8
(8½, 9, 9)"

2"

24
(24½, 25, 25½)"

16
(16, 16, 16½)"

Front/back

18 (20, 22, 24)"

Main body pattern
8-st and 16-row rep

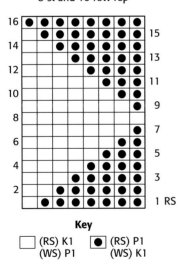

Key

| | (RS) K1 (WS) P1 | ● | (RS) P1 (WS) K1 |

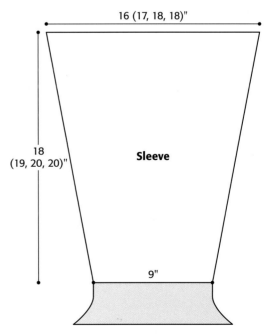

16 (17, 18, 18)"

18
(19, 20, 20)"

Sleeve

9"

Peonies

For this dressy, special-occasion sweater, I chose a luxury yarn, a soft and sumptuous merino-silk blend. This is a worsted-weight yarn, yet it's not in any way bulky in its look or fit. Although it looks complicated, the shell/fan pattern is easy to knit, requiring only knit and purl stitches, yarn overs, and basic decrease stitches. The secret to this pattern is a delayed decrease; in a 10-row pattern repeat, you'll increase every other row (so the number of stitches per row keeps growing) until the end of the pattern repeat, when all the decreases are made in the same row.

Shaping for this sweater is minimal, because the stitch pattern scallops itself and drapes beautifully. I wanted to design an evening sweater that was unequivocally an evening sweater, so in addition to the flashy color array, I added a low-cut, square neckline. This sweater will drape beautifully on any size woman. I can see it paired with a floor-length taffeta skirt or a long, slim velvet skirt or pants. Because you're using a very rich, lightly twisted, heavy yarn for this sweater, you need to be careful not to pull it too much. And, most importantly, it must not be hand washed, but dry-cleaned to avoid being stretched out of shape.

SIZE DETAILS

To Fit Bust Size: 38 (46)"
Finished Bust: 40½ (48½)"
Finished Length: 23½ (25¼)"
Finished Sleeve Length: 11 (11)"

MATERIALS

3 (4) skeins of Lion and Lamb from
Lorna's Laces (50% silk, 50%
merino; 205 yds/3½ oz skein) in
color Vera 〔4〕

1 pair of US size 8 (5 mm) needles or
size to obtain gauge

2 row counters

Stitch markers

Spare needles or stitch holders

GAUGE

4 sts = 1"; 5½ rows = 1" in patt

SHELL/FAN PATTERN

(16-st rep plus 1 st; 10-row rep)
*Note: Not every row of pattern has the same
number of stitches.*

See chart on page 25 or follow pattern-stitch
instructions below.

Row 1 (RS): *K1, YO, (K1, P1) 7 times, K1, YO;
rep from * to last st; K1.

Row 2: K1, *(K1, P1) 8 times, P1, K1; rep from
* to end.

Row 3: *K1, YO, K1, (K1, P1) 7 times, K1, YO,
K1; rep from * to last st, K1.

Row 4: K1, *K1, P2, (K1, P1) 7 times, P1, K2;
rep from * to end.

Row 5: *K3, YO, (K1, P1) 7 times, K1, YO, K2;
rep from * to last st, K1.

Row 6: K1, *K2, P2, (K1, P1) 7 times, P1, K3;
rep from * to end.

Row 7: *K4, YO, (K1, P1) 7 times, K1, YO, K3;
rep from * to last st, K1.

Row 8: K1, *K3, P2, (K1, P1) 7 times, P1, K4;
rep from * to end.

Row 9: K5, *ssk 3 times; sl 1 kw, K2tog, psso
once; K2tog 3 times; K4; rep from * to last
st, K1.

Row 10: Purl.

BACK

- CO 81 (97) sts for 5 (6) horizontal reps plus 1 end st. Place markers between reps.

- Work even until row 5 of the 9th (10th) vertical rep. BO 10 sts at beg of this row. BO 11 sts at beg of next row (row 6 of patt rep).

- Cont working in patt for 13 (14) vertical reps. On last row of patt (row 10) put 17 sts on spare needle for 3-needle BO; BO 26 (42) sts; put remaining 17 sts on spare needle for 3-needle BO.

KEEPING AN ACCURATE COUNT

Although this pattern is made up of basic knit, purl, yarn over, and decrease stitches, it can become confusing if you lose your place in the chart or row directions. To make it easy to always know where you are in your pattern, use one counter to keep track of which pattern row you've just worked, and a second counter to keep track of the number of vertical repeats you've completed.

FRONT

- CO 81 (97) sts for 5 (6) horizontal reps plus 1 end st.

- Work even in patt until row 5 of 9th (10th) vertical rep. On this RS row, BO 10 sts. On next row (row 6 of vertical rep), BO 11 sts.

- Cont working in patt for 10 (11) vertical reps. On last row of patt (row 10), work 17 sts; attach 2nd ball of yarn and BO 26 (42) sts.

- Work 3 more vertical reps for a total of 13 (14) vertical reps. AT SAME TIME, on 9th row, on each of vertical reps 11, 12, and 13 (12, 13, and 14), dec 1 st at each neck edge. After completing last row of rep (row 10), place rem sts on spare needle or st holder.

SLEEVES *(Make 2)*

- CO 49 sts for all sizes (3 horizontal reps plus 1 st).

- Work 6 vertical reps. AT SAME TIME, on 5th row and every subsequent 4th row (RS), inc 1 st in garter st at each sleeve edge 8 times.

- On row 10 of 6th vertical rep, BO loosely.

FINISHING

- Join front and back shoulder sts, using 3-needle BO (see page 12).

- Sew sleeve top to body. Sew underarm and side seams.

- Don't wet or steam this yarn. Dry-clean only.

Peonies chart
16-st rep plus 1-st
10-row rep

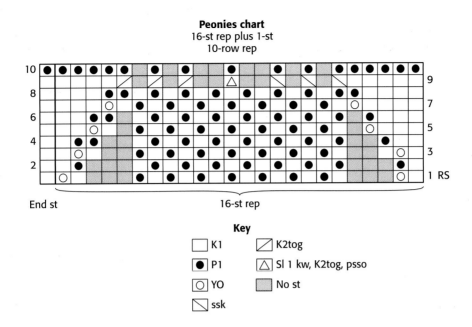

End st   16-st rep

Key

☐	K1	◹	K2tog
●	P1	△	Sl 1 kw, K2tog, psso
○	YO	▨	No st
◺	ssk		

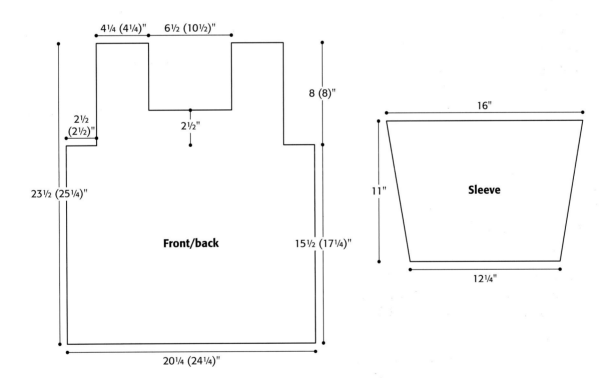

Front/back

Sleeve

Desert Lichen

The colors of this yarn remind me of the desert in summer, so I chose to make a summer tee with a cap sleeve. It's a good design for a variegated yarn because the simple lines show off the color changes. This top has a certain rough, casual look to it that makes it perfect over, say, white pants or shorts for hot weather. However, I can also see it being worn under the unstructured jacket of a winter suit.

SIZE DETAILS

To Fit Bust Size: 34 (38, 42, 46, 50)"
Finished Bust: 36 (40, 44, 48, 52)"
Finished Length: 20 (20, 20, 22, 22)"

MATERIALS

7 (7, 10, 10, 13) skeins of Fantasy Naturale from Plymouth Yarns (100% cotton; 140 yds/100 g skein) in color 9939 Earth Tones **4**

1 pair of US size 7 (4.5 mm) needles or size to obtain gauge

1 set of US size 7 (4.5 mm) double-pointed needles or size 7, 16" circular needle

Stitch holders

GAUGE

4½ sts = 1"; 5 rows = 1" in garter st

BACK

- CO 80 (90, 100, 108, 116) sts. Work 4 rows of K1, P1 rib.

- On next RS row, maintaining 5 sts in rib at each edge, work in garter st (knit all rows). When piece measures 2¾", stop rib at edges and work across entire row in garter st.

- When piece measures 13 (12¾, 12¾, 14½, 14¼)", on next RS row, beg working first and last 5 sts of row in K1, P1 rib, continuing with garter st in between. Cont in this manner until piece measures 20 (20, 20, 22, 22)".

- On next row, BO 20 (25, 30, 34, 38) sts; put next 40 sts on holder; BO 20 (25, 30, 34, 38) sts.

FRONT

- Work as for back until armhole measures 3¼".

- On next RS row, work 5 sts in K1, P1 rib, work next 30 (35, 40, 44, 48) sts in garter, and then work 5 sts in K1, P1 rib. Attach 2nd ball of yarn and work 5 sts in rib, work 30 (35, 40, 44, 48) sts in garter st, and last 5 sts in rib.

- Cont working both sides of neck opening in patt. When armhole measures 7 (7¼, 7¼, 7½, 7¾)", BO 20 (25, 30, 34, 38) sts; put 20 sts on holder; put next 20 sts on 2nd holder; and BO rem 20 (25, 30, 34, 38) sts.

FINISHING

- Sew shoulder seams.

- **Neck:** Place neck sts from holders onto dpns or circular needle, beg at right front edge, and continuing around to left front edge. Work 4 rows back and forth in garter st, maintaining 5 sts in rib at each front neck edge. Then work K1, P1 rib across all sts for 4 rows. BO in ribbing.

- Sew side seams. Weave in ends.

- To block, soak sweater overnight in cold water and baby shampoo. The next day, rinse sweater and put it in washer on spin cycle. Then lay it out flat to dry.

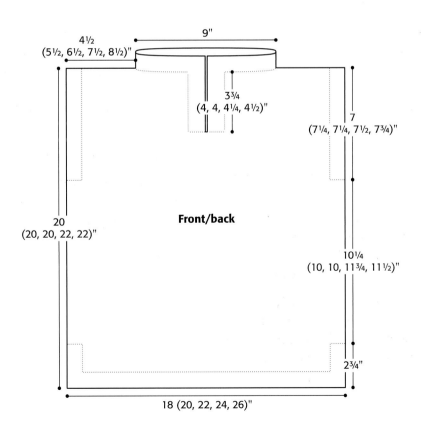

4½
(5½, 6½, 7½, 8½)"

9"

3¾
(4, 4, 4¼, 4½)"

7
(7¼, 7¼, 7½, 7¾)"

20
(20, 20, 22, 22)"

Front/back

10¼
(10, 10, 11¾, 11½)"

2¾"

18 (20, 22, 24, 26)"

Gansey Gold

I updated a traditional gansey design by making the lower half of this sweater a close-fitting rib and giving the upper half a blousy look with time-honored motifs. This sweater has a very flattering fit, especially for larger women. The yarn is a standard four-ply worsted wool, making a garment comfortable enough for home wear, yet pretty enough for the office. A machine-washable wool would make it extremely practical too.

This sweater could also be knit in a worsted-weight cotton or cotton-wool blend. For a dressier look, choose a blend with silk or cashmere or a worsted-weight wool or luxury-blend tweed. You may find some lovely silk tweeds available in the appropriate weight too. This modern gansey is easy to knit, fit, and wear.

SIZE DETAILS

To Fit Bust Size: 38–40 (46–48, 56–58)"
Finished Bust: 44 (53, 63)"
Finished Length: 24 (25, 26)"
Finished Sleeve Length: 18 (18½, 19)"

MATERIALS

14 (18, 22) balls of Heilo from Dale of Norway (100% wool; 110 yds/50 g ball) in color 2427 Gold ⟨3⟩

1 pair of US size 4 (3.5 mm) needles or size to obtain gauge

1 set of US size 4 (3.5 mm) double-pointed needles

Stitch markers

Spare needles or stitch holders

GAUGE

6 sts = 1"; 8 rows = 1" in patt

PATTERNS

See charts A and B on page 34 or follow the written row directions below.

Pattern A
(13-st and 16-row rep)

Row 1 (RS): P5, K3, P5.

Row 2: K5, P3, K5.

Row 3: P4, K2, P1, K2, P4.

Row 4: K4, P2, K1, P2, K4.

Row 5: P3, K2, P1, K1, P1, K2, P3.

Row 6: K3, P2, K1, P1, K1, P2, K3.

Row 7: P2, K2, (P1, K1) twice, P1, K2, P2.

Row 8: K2, P2, (K1, P1) twice, K1, P2, K2.

Row 9: P1, K2, (P1, K1) 4 times, K1, P1.

Row 10: K1, P2, (K1, P1) 4 times, P1, K1.

Row 11: Rep row 7.

Row 12: Rep row 8.

Row 13: Rep row 5.

Row 14: Rep row 6.

Row 15: Rep row 3.

Row 16: Rep row 4.

Pattern B
(16-st and 4-row rep)

Row 1 (RS): K2, P5, K2, P5, K2.

Row 2: P2, K5, P2, K5, P2.

Row 3: Knit.

Row 4: Purl.

BACK

- CO 132 (158, 190) sts. Work in K2, P2 rib for 12 (12½, 13)".

- On next WS row, knit across.

- On next RS row, beg A and B patt layout from charts or directions above as follows, placing markers between each A and B section.
  For first size: B, A, B, A, B, A, B, A, B.
  For second size: A, B, A, B, A, B, A, B, A, B, A.
  For third size: B, A, B, A, B, A, B, A, B, A, B, A, B.

- Work in patt until upper section measures 11½ (12, 12½)".

- On next RS row, work 39 (49, 62) sts; attach 2nd ball of yarn and BO 54 (60, 66) sts; work rem 39 (49, 62) sts. Cont in patt until upper section measures 12 (12½, 13)".

- Place shoulder sts on spare needles or st holders.

FRONT

- Work as for back until patt section measures 9" for all sizes.

- On next RS row, work 43 (52, 65) sts; attach 2nd ball of yarn and BO 46 (54, 60) sts; work rem 43 (52, 65) sts.

- On next and following RS rows, dec 1 st at each neck edge 4 times for all sizes—35 (44, 57) sts. Work even until patt section measures 12 (12½, 13)".

- Place shoulder sts on spare needles or st holders.

SLEEVES (*Make 2*)

- CO 48 (52, 56) sts. Work in K2, P2 rib. AT SAME TIME, on 5th and every subsequent 4th row (RS), inc 1 st at each sleeve edge 27 (28, 29) times—102 (108, 114) sts.

- When sleeve measures 18 (18½, 19)", BO all sts loosely.

FINISHING

- Join front and back shoulder sts, using 3-needle BO (see page 12).

- Using dpns, beg at left shoulder seam, PU 1 of every 2 sts on diagonals, 2 of every 3 sts on front neck BO, and 3 of every 4 sts on back neck BO. The K2, P2 rib has a 4-st rep. If total number of sts you picked up isn't divisible by 4, adjust number of sts around neck on first row of patt at left shoulder.

- Work in K2, P2 rib for 1½".

- To sew in sleeves, mark armhole depth—8½ (9, 9½)"—on sweater body on both sides of shoulder seam.

- Stretch sleeve top evenly between markers, pin, and sew seam. Sew underarm and side seams. Weave in ends.

- No special blocking is required.

Gansey Gold chart A
13-st and 16-row rep

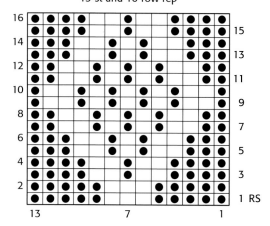

Gansey Gold chart B
16-st and 4-row rep

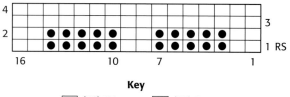

Key

☐ (RS) K1 (WS) P1	⬤ (RS) P1 (WS) K1

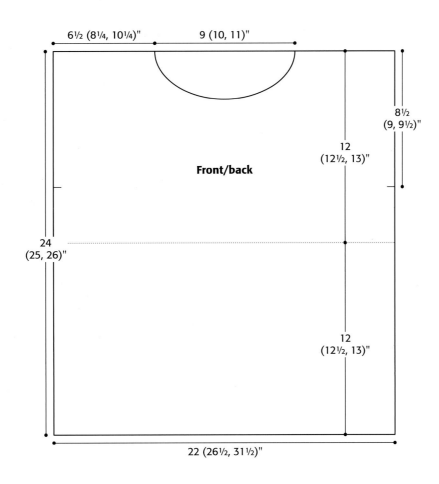

6½ (8¼, 10¼)"   9 (10, 11)"

8½ (9, 9½)"

12 (12½, 13)"

Front/back

24 (25, 26)"

12 (12½, 13)"

22 (26½, 31½)"

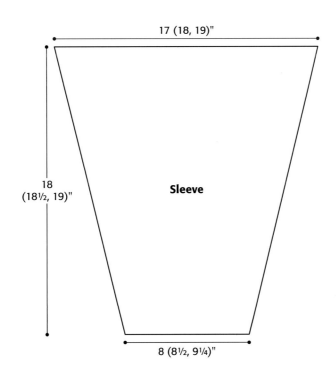

17 (18, 19)"

18 (18½, 19)"

Sleeve

8 (8½, 9¼)"

Highland Mist

I couldn't resist including a lace shawl in this collection. It's one that could even be matched to and worn with a number of the sweaters in this book. You may recognize the traditional Shetland lace pattern called Crest o' the Wave—it's one of my favorites. For this shawl, I used a hand-painted yarn, a very fine lace-weight merino/silk blend. While this design would look nice knit in a high-contrast, hand-painted yarn, I personally prefer the look of a more subtle blend of colors as shown here. To me it's more sophisticated and less showy. You could also use a solid-color lace yarn quite successfully.

Blocking is important to give a good look to this piece. Don't be tempted to skip that step or be alarmed that your shawl doesn't look quite like the picture as you're knitting it. It's not until after it's blocked that the true beauty of the lace pattern is completely revealed. This design is extremely easy to knit, so don't be turned away by small needles and fine yarn. They work!

FINISHED SIZE

Measurements are after blocking.

16" x 60", plus 14" of tassels

MATERIALS

1 skein of hand-painted, fine lace yarn
from Skaska Designs (50% merino,
50% silk; 1,260 yds) in color Blue-
Periwinkle ⓵

1 pair of US size 1 (2.25 mm) 10"-long
needles or size to obtain gauge

Stitch markers

2 row counters

Small crochet hook

GAUGE

11 sts = 1"; 7 rows = 1"; blocked, in patt

LACE PATTERN

12-st rep plus 3 end sts, 16-row rep

See pattern chart at top right or follow the
written row directions below.

Row 1 (RS): Sl 1, knit to end.

Row 2 and all even-numbered rows: Sl 1, knit
to end.

Rows 3, 5, 7, 9, 11, and 13 (RS): Sl 1, K1, PM,
*K2tog twice, (YO, K1) 3 times, YO, ssk
twice, K1, PM; rep from * to last st, K1.

Row 15: Sl 1, knit to end.

Row 16: Knit.

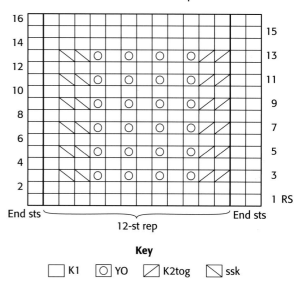

Crest o' the Wave chart
12-st and 16-row rep

Key

☐ K1	⊙ YO	⟋ K2tog	⟍ ssk

SHAWL

- CO 171 sts. Work 2 rows of garter st.

- On next RS row, beg patt row 1 as follows:
  K2, PM, work 14 patt reps, placing a marker
  between each rep, K1. To keep track of
  your rows and vertical reps, try using 2
  counters—1 for individual rows within a
  rep and 1 for the number of the rep you're
  currently working on.

- Cont in patt, working 27 vertical reps.

- Work 2 rows of garter st.

- BO all sts loosely.

A FINE EDGE

Because the lace-weight yarn is so fine,
you can give your shawl a nice, smooth,
yet stretchy edge by slipping the first
stitch of each row. Slip as if to purl on
both right and wrong sides of the work.
This is important for blocking.

FINISHING

- To block lace, soak shawl overnight in cold water. Roll up in towel to remove excess moisture. On large, flat surface, pin out piece to finished dimensions given below. Ends will be deeply scalloped.

- Cut yarn into 120 pieces, 16" long, for tassels. Using 4 pieces for each tassel, fold pieces in half lengthwise and use crochet hook to pull folded strands through edge of shawl at center of scallop. Loop ends through folded edge and pull tight. Make tassel at center of each scallop—15 on each end of shawl.

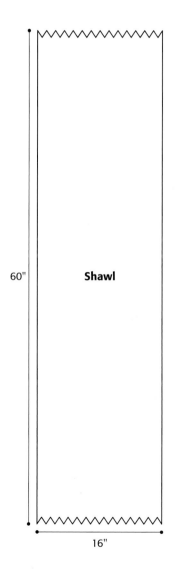

60"

Shawl

16"

Mrs. Laidlaw's Pattern

This is the ultimate classic pullover in my collection. It's done in a fingering-weight wool to make it both lightweight and dressy. Although the repeat is quite large, the sweater is only moderately difficult to knit, because the only stitches used are knit and purl. A straightedge will help you read the charts so that you don't become lost. Row counters are vital—one for the rows within the repeat and another for the number of repeats.

This design is modeled after a 19th-century fisherman gansey from Seahouses, a small coastal town in northern England. The pattern, which is known by the name of its originator, Mrs. Laidlaw, features soft shaping and lots of verticality. Personally, I love the classics; I feel that traditional designs transcend the vagaries of style and look great on everyone. This particular sweater is suitable for advanced or adventurous beginners and beyond, and will be a knitting accomplishment that is sure to become a favored garment in your wardrobe. If you live in a warm climate, try substituting a fingering-weight cotton, such as Dale of Norway Stork, for the lightweight wool.

SIZE DETAILS

To Fit Bust Size: 40–42 (47–49)"
Finished Bust: 46½ (53)"
Finished Length: 26½ (26½)"
Finished Sleeve Length: 20 (21)"

MATERIALS

8 (10) balls of Baby Ull from Dale of
 Norway (100% superwash merino
 wool; 191 yds/50 g ball) in color
 5303 Lavender 🧶1

1 pair of US size 2 (2.75 mm) needles or
 size to obtain gauge

1 set of US size 2 (2.75 mm) double-
 pointed needles

Spare needles or stitch holders

Stitch markers

2 row counters

GAUGE

6 sts =1"; 8¾ rows = 1" in patt

PATTERNS

Pattern A
See chart on page 45.

Pattern B
See chart on page 45.

Seed Stitch
(2-st, 2-row rep)

Row 1 (RS): *K1, P1; rep from * to end.

Row 2 (WS): *P1, K1; rep from * to end.

Rib Pattern
(4-st rep)

All rows: *K2, P2; rep from * to end.

BACK

- CO 136 (156) sts. Work rib patt for 2". On last WS row, inc 3 sts across: 139 (159) sts. Reading from charts, beg patt layout on next RS row as follows. Place markers between each patt section for easier knitting.

  For smaller size: B, A, B, A, B.
  For larger size: Work 10 sts in seed st, B, A, B, A, B, work last 10 sts in seed st.

- Work even in est patt until you've completed 5 vertical reps of chart A.

- On next RS row, work across in seed st, inc 1 st at center of row: 140 (160) sts. Cont to work in seed st for 2½".

- On next RS row, work 43 (51) sts; attach 2nd ball of yarn and BO 54 (58) sts; work rem 43 (51) sts. When seed-st section measures 3", put shoulder sts on spare needle or holder for 3-needle BO.

FRONT

- Work as for back until top seed-st section measures ½".

- On next RS row, work 51 (59) sts; attach 2nd ball of yarn and BO 38 (42) sts; work 51 (59) sts.

- Work dec on each edge of neck as follows: BO 2 sts 3 times; dec 1 st 2 times.

- When seed-st section measures 3", put shoulder sts on spare needle or holder for 3-needle BO.

SLEEVES *(Make 2)*

- CO 54 (54) sts. Work rib patt for 2". On last WS row, inc 1 st: 55 sts.

- On next RS row, work 4 sts in seed st, work 1 rep of patt A, work last 4 sts in seed st.

- Cont working in est patt. AT SAME TIME, on 5th and every subsequent 4th row (RS), inc 1 st at each sleeve edge in seed st 32 times: 120 sts.

- Work even until you complete 4 vertical reps of patt A.

- On next RS row, change to seed st and work across. When seed-st section measures 1", BO loosely.

FINISHING

- Join front and back shoulder sts, using 3-needle BO (see page 12).

- Beg at left shoulder, use dpns to PU 1 of every 2 sts on diagonals, PU 2 of every 3 sts on front neck BO, PU 3 of every 4 sts on back neck BO. You'll need an even number of sts, so if you need to add a st, do so on left shoulder. Work in the round in seed st for 1". BO very loosely.

- Sew sleeve tops to body. Sew underarm and side seams. Weave in ends.

- Soak sweater overnight in cold water. Put it in washer on spin cycle to remove excess moisture. Then lay sweater out on flat surface and gently shape edges until pattern lies flat. (Don't stretch!) Let dry. This yarn is machine-washable.

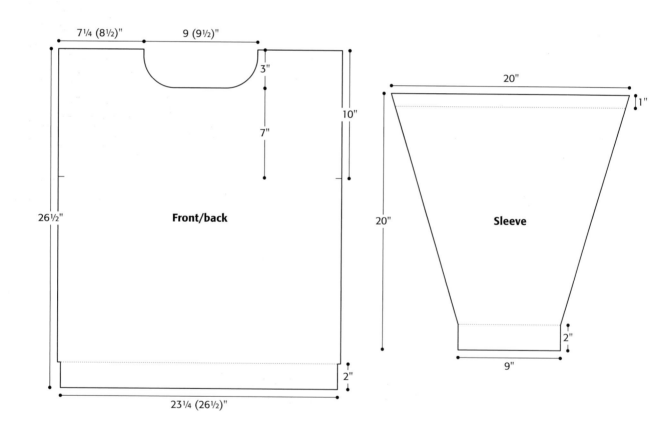

Mrs. Laidlaw's Pattern chart A
47-st and 36-row rep

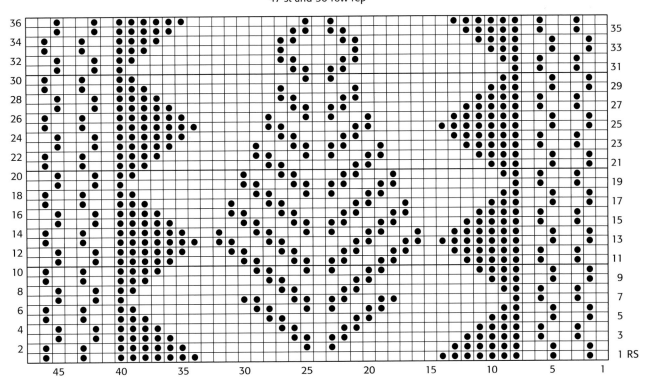

Mrs. Laidlaw's Pattern chart B
15-st and 12-row rep

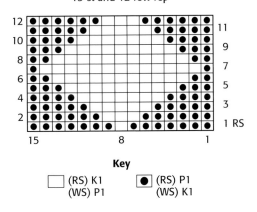

Key

☐ (RS) K1 (WS) P1	● (RS) P1 (WS) K1

Spring Surprise

I designed this fitted vest with my teenage niece in mind, so it has a very youthful look. It knits up quickly in a chunky-weight novelty yarn that self-finishes the edges. Rather than try to make buttonholes, I just threaded the ribbons through the fabric with a large-eyed needle. They don't need to be undone to put the vest on, because even with the ribbons tied, this vest will easily slip over the head. For washing, simply remove the ribbons. An alternative closure might be frogs or large buttons with loops, either of which would tone down the look. Being extremely easy to knit, this vest is suitable for a first-time knitter.

SIZE DETAILS

To Fit Bust Size: 28–30 (32–34, 36–38, 40–42)"
Finished Bust: 32 (36, 40, 44)"
Finished Length: 19¼ (19½, 20¾, 21)"

MATERIALS

5 (6, 7, 8) skeins of Mineral from Plassard (35% wool, 35% polyamide, 30% acrylic; 72 yds/50 g skein) in color 56 Blue Pink

1 pair of US size 10 (6 mm) needles or size to obtain gauge

2 yds of ½"-wide satin ribbon in Rose

Sewing thread

GAUGE

3¼" sts = 1"; 6 rows = 1" in garter st

BACK

- CO 53 (59, 65, 71) sts. Work in garter st throughout (knit all rows).

- When piece measures 2 (2, 2½, 2½)", dec 1 st at each edge. When piece measures 3 (3, 3½, 3½)", dec 1 st at each edge. When piece measures 4 (4, 4½, 4½)", dec 1 st at each edge: 47 (53, 59, 65) sts rem.

- When piece measures 6 (6, 6½, 6½)", inc 1 st at each edge. When piece measures 7 (7, 7½, 7½)", inc 1 st at each edge. When piece measures 8 (8, 8½, 8½)", inc 1 st at each edge: 53 (59, 65, 71) sts.

- Work even until piece measures 12 (12, 13, 13)". BO 5 sts at beg of next 2 rows for armholes.

- Work even until armholes measure 5¼ (5½, 5¾, 6)". On next RS row, work 7 (9, 11, 13) sts; attach 2nd ball of yarn and BO 29 (31, 33, 35) sts; work rem 7 (9, 11, 13) sts. Cont working both shoulders even until armhole measures 7¼ (7½, 7¾, 8)". BO shoulder sts.

RIGHT FRONT

- CO 45 (51, 56, 62) sts. Work in same manner as for back, but make all side dec, inc, and BO *on right edge only*.

- When armhole measures as for back, on RS, work 4 (6, 7, 9) sts; attach 2nd ball of yarn and BO 29 (31, 33, 35) sts; work rem 7 (9, 11, 13) sts.

- When armhole measures as for back, BO shoulder sts.

LEFT FRONT

- CO 12 (14, 16, 18) sts. Work in same manner as for back but make all edge dec, inc, and BO *on left edge only.*

- Cont to work even after armhole BO until armhole measures as for back. BO shoulder sts.

FINISHING

- Using sewing thread and overcast st, sew right front shoulder to right back shoulder. Sew left front shoulder to left back shoulder. Sew side seams. Weave in ends. To overcast, insert needle from front edge and pull thread through to back. Bring needle from back over edges of knitting and insert into next st on front. Rep this for every st.

- Cut five 14" lengths of ribbon. To add ribbon closures, lay right front over left front. (Note that the left shoulder portion of right front is narrower than left front.) The 2 pieces should overlap about 1". Thread ribbon through a st on left front so that both ribbon tails are visible on top of sweater, not on inside. Then thread 1 end through edge of right front as shown in photograph below. Tie ends together in bow and trim ends diagonally. Rep, placing bow at top of shoulder, bottom bow about 1" from bottom, and other bows evenly spaced in between.

- No blocking is required.

- Because bows aren't sewn in place, they can easily be removed before washing.

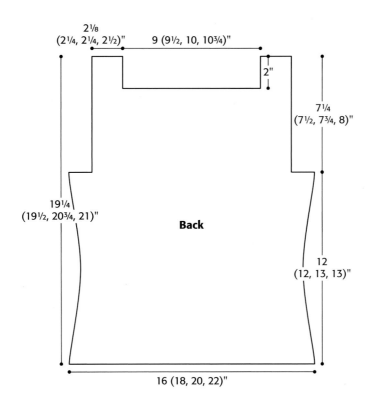

2⅛
(2¼, 2¼, 2½)"   9 (9½, 10, 10¾)"

2"

7¼
(7½, 7¾, 8)"

19¼
(19½, 20¾, 21)"

Back

12
(12, 13, 13)"

16 (18, 20, 22)"

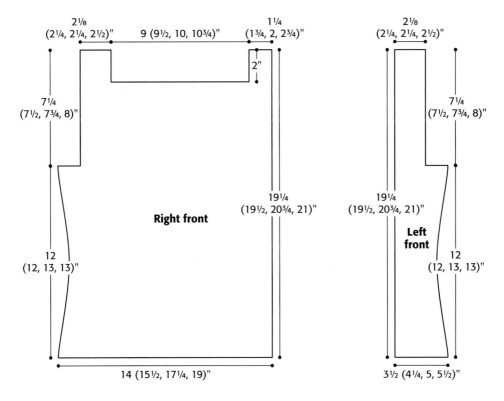

2⅛
(2¼, 2¼, 2½)"   9 (9½, 10, 10¾)"   1¼
(1¾, 2, 2¾)"

2⅛
(2¼, 2¼, 2½)"

2"

7¼
(7½, 7¾, 8)"

7¼
(7½, 7¾, 8)"

19¼
(19½, 20¾, 21)"

19¼
(19½, 20¾, 21)"

Right front

**Left
front**

12
(12, 13, 13)"

12
(12, 13, 13)"

14 (15½, 17¼, 19)"

3½ (4¼, 5, 5½)"

Sand and Shore

Some cardigans are sporty and rugged—great for outdoor wear. Others are dressier and can substitute for a suit jacket. Here is one that's in between, with both a dressy look and a comfortable fit. Not only is this sweater one of my favorites to wear, it's one of my favorites to knit. True to my goal as a designer, this sweater looks complicated, yet the large pattern repeat and seed-stitch borders are extremely simple to knit. Because only knit and purl stitches are used, this pattern is accessible to confident beginners.

The DK-weight wool yarn has a firm hand, making this a good learning project without looking like one. The design is classic and sophisticated and, with a muted heather color and strong verticality, it's flattering for all sizes. As I do with all cardigans, to facilitate a comfortable fit, I make the front slightly wider than the back and allow for roomy armholes and sleeves. You could substitute a cotton or cotton-wool blend for this wool as long as you select a yarn that's firmly twisted, so the pattern work will stand out.

SIZE DETAILS

To Fit Bust Size: 34 (38, 44, 48)"
Finished Bust: 38½ (43¼, 48, 52¾)"
Finished Length: 26 (27, 28, 28)"
Finished Sleeve Length: 19 (20, 20, 21)"

MATERIALS

17 (17, 19, 21) skeins of Jamieson's
    Shetland DK from Unicorn Books
    and Crafts Inc. (100% wool;
    82 yds/25 g skein) in color
    290 Oyster 🄷

1 pair of US size 4 (3.5 mm) needles or
    size to obtain gauge

Stitch markers

Spare needles or stitch holders

11 (11, 12, 12) buttons, 1" diameter

GAUGE

5 sts = 1"; 6½ rows = 1" in patt

PATTERNS

Seed Stitch
(2-st, 2-row rep)

Row 1 (RS): *K1, P1; rep from * to end.

Row 2: *P1, K1; rep from * to end.

Main Body Pattern
(12-st, 20-row rep)

See chart on page 56, or follow written pattern
    repeat below.

Row 1 (RS): *K6, P6, rep from * to end.

Row 2: *P1, K5, P5, K1, rep from * to end.

Row 3: *P2, K4, P4, K2, rep from * to end.

Row 4: *P3, K3, P3, K3, rep from * to end.

Row 5: *K1, P3, K2, P2, K3, P1, rep from * to end.

Row 6: *K2, P3, K1, P1, K3, P2, rep from * to end.

Row 7: *K3, P3, K3, P3, rep from * to end.

Row 8: *K4, P2, K2, P4, rep from * to end.

Row 9: *K5, P1, K1, P5, rep from * to end.

Row 10: *K6, P6, rep from * to end.

Row 11: *K6, P6, rep from * to end.

Row 12: *K5, P1, K1, P5, rep from * to end.

Row 13: *K4, P2, K2, P4, rep from * to end.

Row 14: *K3, P3, K3, P3, rep from * to end.

Row 15: *K2, P3, K1, P1, K3, P2, rep from * to end.

Row 16: *K1, P3, K2, P2, K3, P1, rep from * to end.

Row 17: *P3, K3, P3, K3, rep from * to end.

Row 18: *P2, K4, P4, K2, rep from * to end.

Row 19: *P1, K5, P5, K1, rep from * to end.

Row 20: *K6, P6, rep from * to end.

BACK

- CO 96 (108, 120, 132) sts. Work in seed st for 1½".

- On next RS row, beg main body patt. You will work 8 (9, 10, 11) horizontal reps across. Place markers between patt sections.

- Work even in patt until piece measures 16½ (17, 17½, 17½)", ending on WS row.

- At beg of next 2 rows, BO 6 sts for all sizes. Work even in patt until armhole measures 9 (9½, 10, 10)".

- On next RS row, work 19 (24, 30, 35) sts; attach 2nd ball of yarn and BO 46 (48, 48, 50) sts; work rem 19 (24, 30, 35) sts. Cont in patt until armhole measures 9½ (10, 10½, 10½)".

- Place shoulder sts on spare needle or st holders for 3-needle BO.

LEFT FRONT

- CO 48 (54, 60, 66) sts. Work in seed st for 1½".

- On next RS row, beg main body patt. You will work 4 (4½, 5, 5½) horizontal reps across. Place markers between patt sections.

- Work even in patt until piece measures 16½ (17, 17½, 17½)", ending on WS row.

- At beg of next RS row, BO 6 sts for all sizes. Work even in patt until armhole measures 6¾ (7, 7¼, 7¼)", ending on a RS row.

- On next and following WS rows, BO 2 sts at neck edge 3 times, then dec 1 st at neck edge 3 times. Work even until armhole measures 9½ (10, 10½, 10½)".

- Place shoulder sts on spare needle or st holders for 3-needle BO.

RIGHT FRONT

- CO 48 (54, 60, 66) sts. Work in seed st for 1½".

- On next RS row, beg main body patt, starting at row 1, st 7. Work even in patt until piece measures as for left front.

- At beg of next WS row, BO 6 sts. Work even in patt until armhole measures 6¾ (7, 7¼, 7¼)", ending on a WS row.

- On next and following RS rows, BO 2 sts at neck edge 3 times, then dec 1 st at neck edge 3 times. Work even until armhole measures 9½ (10, 10½, 10½)".

- Place shoulder sts on spare needle or st holders for 3-needle BO.

SLEEVES (Make 2)

- CO 60 (60, 60, 60) sts. Work in seed st for 1½".

- On next RS row, beg main body patt, beg with row 1, st 7. Place markers between patt sections.

- Work in patt. AT SAME TIME, on 5th and every subsequent 4th row (RS), inc 1 st at each sleeve edge 18 (20, 23, 23) times: 96 (100, 106, 106) sts total.

- Work even in patt until sleeve measures 19 (20, 20, 21)". BO all sts.

FINISHING

- Join front and back shoulder sts, using 3-needle BO (see page 12).

- **Neckband:** PU 1 of every 2 sts on diagonals, 2 of every 3 sts on front neck BO, and 3 of every 4 sts on back neck BO. Work in seed st for 1½". BO loosely.

- **Left front band:** On left front edge, PU 3 of every 4 sts. Work in seed st for 1½". BO loosely.

- **Right front band:** On right front edge, PU 3 of every 4 sts. Work in seed st for ¾". On next RS row, work desired number of buttonholes. Work first and last buttonhole ½" from top and bottom edges, spacing rem buttonholes evenly between them. Buttonholes are worked over 4 sts as follows: On RS, K2tog, YO, YO, K2tog. On WS, K1, P1, K1, P1. Resume seed-st patt on next RS row and work for ¾". BO loosely.

- Sew buttons to left front band.

- Sew underarm and side seams.

- No blocking is required.

Sand and Shore main body pattern
12-st and 20-row rep

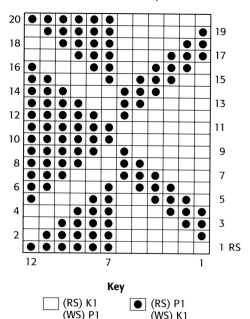

Key

☐ (RS) K1 (WS) P1	● (RS) P1 (WS) K1

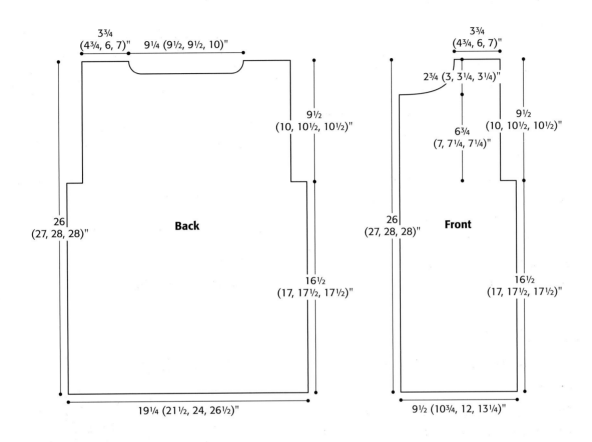

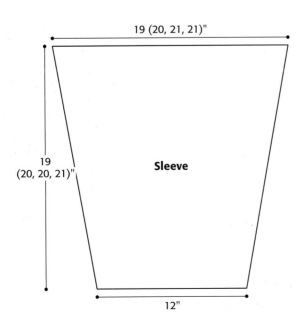

Back

3¾
(4¾, 6, 7)"   9¼ (9½, 9½, 10)"

9½
(10, 10½, 10½)"

26
(27, 28, 28)"

16½
(17, 17½, 17½)"

19¼ (21½, 24, 26½)"

Front

3¾
(4¾, 6, 7)"

2¾ (3, 3¼, 3¼)"

9½
(10, 10½, 10½)"

6¾
(7, 7¼, 7¼)"

26
(27, 28, 28)"

16½
(17, 17½, 17½)"

9½ (10¾, 12, 13¼)"

Sleeve

19 (20, 21, 21)"

19
(20, 20, 21)"

12"

Pralines and Cream

I was intrigued with this chunky thick-and-thin yarn from Dale of Norway when I first saw it. I love winter white, and this is definitely a cold-weather sweater. The boxy shape and lack of fussy detail allow the yarn to shine. These factors also make the sweater extremely easy to knit and comfortable to wear. The design is definitely casual and would be great for outdoor wear or for just sitting around the fireplace on a winter evening.

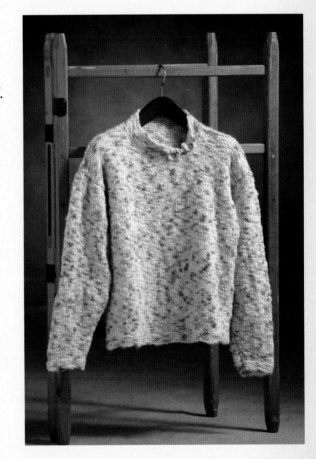

SIZE DETAILS

To Fit Bust Size: 32 (36, 40, 44, 48)"
Finished Bust: 36 (40, 44, 48, 52)"
Finished Length: 23 (23½, 24, 24½, 25)"
Finished Sleeve Length: 19 (20, 20, 21, 21)"

MATERIALS

16 (18, 20, 22, 24) balls of Ara from Dale of Norway (100% wool; 55 yds/50 g ball) in color 404 Pralines and Cream (5)

1 pair of US size 7 (4.5 mm) needles or size to obtain gauge

1 set of US size 7 (4.5 mm) double-pointed needles or size 7, 16" circular needle

Spare needles or stitch holders

2 buttons, ½" diameter

GAUGE

4 sts = 1"; 6 rows = 1"

BACK

- With straight needles, CO 72 (80, 88, 96, 104) sts. Work in garter st for 1". Change to St st and work even until piece measures 15½ (15½, 15½, 16, 16)", ending on WS row.

- At beg of next 2 rows, BO 6 sts for all sizes.

- Work even until armhole measures 7 (7½, 8, 8, 8½)".

- On next RS row, work 15 (19, 22, 26, 28) sts; attach 2nd ball of yarn and BO 30 (30, 32, 32, 36) sts; work rem 15 (19, 22, 26, 28) sts.

- When armhole measures 7½ (8, 8½, 8½, 9)", place shoulder sts on spare needle or st holders for 3-needle BO.

FRONT

- Work same as for back until armhole measures 5 (5½, 6, 6, 6½)".

- On next RS row, work 18 (22, 25, 29, 31) sts; attach 2nd ball of yarn and BO 24 (24, 26, 26, 30) sts; work rem 18 (22, 25, 29, 31) sts.

- On next and following RS rows, dec 1 st at each neck edge 3 times.

- When armhole measures as for back, place shoulder sts on spare needles or st holders for 3-needle BO.

SLEEVES (Make 2)

- With straight needles, CO 36 sts for all sizes. Work in garter st for 1".

- Change to St st. AT SAME TIME, on 5th and every subsequent 4th row (RS), inc 1 st at each sleeve edge 12 (14, 16, 16, 18) times. Total sts: 60 (64, 68, 68, 72).

- When sleeve measures 19 (20, 20, 21, 21)", BO all sts.

FINISHING

- Join front and back shoulder sts, using 3-needle BO (see page 12).

- **Neck:** With dpn or circular needle, PU sts, beg at point where left neck diagonal joins front neck BO. This will be your neck opening. PU 1 of every 2 sts on diagonals, 2 of every 3 sts on front neck BO, and 3 of every 4 sts on back neck BO. Knitting back and forth, *not* in the round, work in garter st. At opening, use right-hand needle to PU 4 sts behind and below sts on end of left-hand needle. Start your row here. At end of row with left-hand needle, PU 4 sts in front of and below sts on right-hand needle. Turn and work back. Work until neck measures 2". BO all sts loosely.

- Fold corners of neck down and anchor each corner to sweater front with button.

- Sew underarm and side seams. Weave in ends.

- **Blocking:** Soak overnight in cold water; then roll in towels to remove excess moisture. Lay out on flat surface to dry and use T-pins to anchor garter-st edges so that they don't roll up.

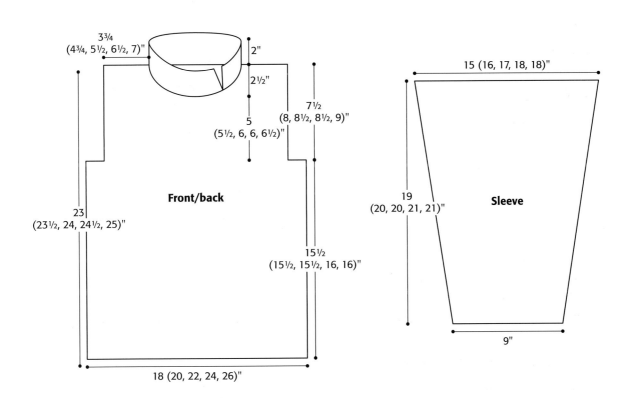

Front/back

3¾
(4¾, 5½, 6½, 7)"

2"

2½"

7½
(8, 8½, 8½, 9)"

5
(5½, 6, 6, 6½)"

23
(23½, 24, 24½, 25)"

15½
(15½, 15½, 16, 16)"

18 (20, 22, 24, 26)"

Sleeve

15 (16, 17, 18, 18)"

19
(20, 20, 21, 21)"

9"

Tweed Comfort

When I think of tweed, I think of a somewhat oversized and very comfortable sweater, so for this design, I chose to do an unstructured, roomy pullover with a scrunchy turtleneck. I experimented with different stitch patterns and found that a simple knit/purl moss stitch really shows off the flecks of color and the tweediness of this rich purple DK-weight wool yarn.

This sweater is definitely an easy knit that could be a successful project for a beginner, and it's highly wearable for both the office and at home. In this case, simplicity is sophistication. Sometimes it's best to just let the yarn do the talking!

SIZE DETAILS

To Fit Bust Size: 32 (38, 44, 50)"
Finished Bust: 38 (44, 50, 56)"
Finished Length: 24 (24½, 25, 25½)"
Finished Sleeve Length: 18 (18, 19, 19)"

MATERIALS

8 (10, 12, 14) balls of Sisik from
  Dale of Norway (30% wool, 30%
  mohair, 34% acrylic, 6% viscose;
  148 yds/50 g ball) in color 1031
  Purple Tweed

1 pair of US size 4 (3.5 mm) needles or
  size to obtain gauge

1 set of US size 4 (3.5 mm) double-
  pointed needles or size 4, 16"
  circular needle

Stitch holders

GAUGE

4½ sts = 1"; 8 rows = 1" in patt

MOSS STITCH

(2-st, 4-row rep)

Row 1 (RS): *K1, P1; rep from * to end.

Row 2: *K1, P1; rep from * to end.

Row 3: *P1, K1; rep from * to end.

Row 4: *P1, K1; rep from * to end.

BACK AND FRONT *(Make 2)*

- With straight needles, CO 86 (100, 112, 126)
  sts. Work in moss st until piece measures 24
  (24½, 25, 25½)", ending on WS row.

- At beg of next 2 rows, BO 21 (28, 34, 41) sts.
  Put rem 44 center sts on holder.

SLEEVES *(Make 2)*

- With straight needles, CO 36 sts for all sizes.
  Work in moss st. AT SAME TIME, on 5th
  and every subsequent 4th row, inc 1 st at
  each sleeve edge 23 (25, 27, 29) times: 82 (86,
  90, 94) sts.

- When sleeve measures 18 (18, 19, 19)", BO
  all sts.

FINISHING

- Sew shoulder seams.

- **Neck:** Place front and back neck sts from holders onto dpns or circular needle. Work in moss st. You will be working in the round, so all rows become RS rows. In other words, work row 1 of patt twice, then row 3 twice, and rep. When neck measures 10", BO all sts loosely.

- Sew sleeve tops to body. Sew underarm and side seams. Weave in ends.

- No blocking is necessary.

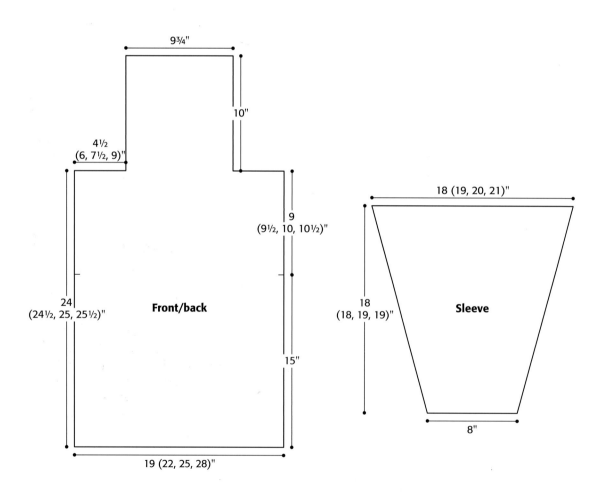

Sea and Seashells

This is a seaside design, incorporating the colors of the Mediterranean and a heavily textured stitch reminiscent of shells on a beach. The simple boatneck complements the ornate patterning and continues the nautical theme. This pattern only *looks* complicated— it's easy to knit and is related to the pattern used in Peonies shown on page 21.

The shaping is loose and casual with simple lines so the pattern can show itself off well. Between the softly variegated colors and the textured stitch pattern, it's the kind of sweater that draws the eye into the details rather than having the viewer focus on the overall dimensions. Therefore, it's a good design for all sizes and body shapes.

I knit this sweater in a wool yarn with a tight twist, which lends itself to heavily textured work. This sweater would also be perfect in a worsted cotton, but choose a crisply twisted cotton yarn to make the pattern stand out.

SIZE DETAILS

To Fit Bust Size: 36 (44, 52)"
Finished Bust: 41 (49, 57)"
Finished Length: 22 (24, 26)"
Finished Sleeve Length: 16½
    (18½, 20½)"

MATERIALS

3 (4, 5) skeins of Fisherman from
    Lorna's Laces (100% wool;
    500 yds/approx 8 oz skein) in color
    42 Cool ⟨3⟩

1 pair of US size 6 (4 mm) needles or
    size to obtain gauge

1 medium-small crochet hook

Stitch markers

GAUGE

4½ sts = 1"; 8 rows = 1" in shell patt

PATTERNS

Garter Stitch
All rows: Knit

Shell Pattern
(9-st rep plus 3 sts)

See chart on page 72.

BACK AND FRONT (Make 2)

- CO 93 (111, 129) sts. Work 6 rows of St st.

- On next RS row, beg shell patt from chart on page 72. Work 1 beg st, work 10 (12, 14) 9-st horizontal reps, work 2 end sts. PM between patt sections.

- Work 21 (23, 25) vertical reps of shell patt chart.

- Work K1, P1 rib for ½".

- BO all sts.

SLEEVES *(Make 2)*

- CO 57 sts for all sizes. Work 6 rows in St st.

- On next RS row, beg shell patt. Work 1 beg st, 6 patt reps, and 2 end sts. AT SAME TIME, on 5th and every subsequent 4th row, inc 1 st in garter st at each sleeve edge 12 (14, 17) times: 81 (85, 91) sts total.

- Work 16 (18, 20) vertical patt reps. BO all sts.

FINISHING

- Measure top edges of front and back, dividing them into 3 sections as follows: 5¼ (6¾, 8¼)" for shoulder; 10 (11, 12)" for neck opening; 5¼ (6¾, 8¼)" for shoulder.

- With wrong sides together, single crochet shoulders together, leaving center sections open for neck.

- Sew sleeve tops to body. Sew underarm and side seams. Weave in ends.

- No blocking is necessary.

Sea and Seashells chart
Note: There are a different number of stitches in each row.

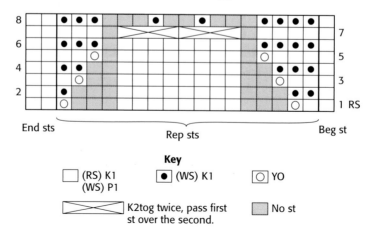

End sts   Rep sts   Beg st

Key

☐ (RS) K1 (WS) P1   ⬛• (WS) K1   ⊙ YO

⧅ K2tog twice, pass first st over the second.   ▨ No st

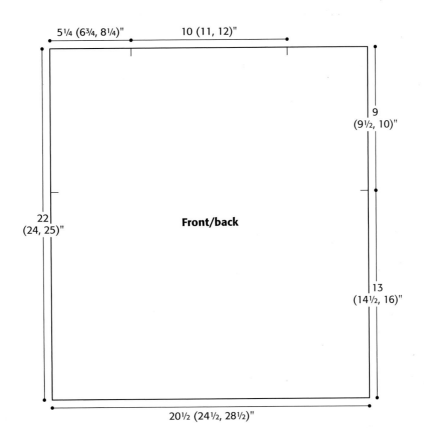

5¼ (6¾, 8¼)"   10 (11, 12)"

9
(9½, 10)"

22
(24, 25)"

Front/back

13
(14½, 16)"

20½ (24½, 28½)"

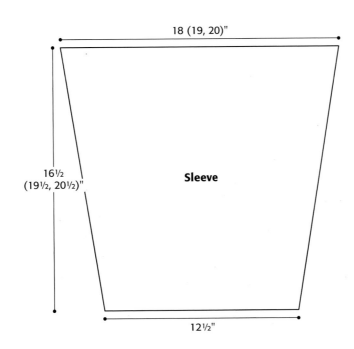

18 (19, 20)"

16½
(19½, 20½)"

Sleeve

12½"

Blue Hawaii

Blue Hawaii combines a bottom lace panel and a lace turtleneck with a plain body. It's a design that looks more difficult to knit than it really is. The straightforward directions are well within the skill range of an advanced beginner or intermediate knitter. The yarn is a lovely DK-weight blend of silk and rayon, hand painted in deep sea colors. This sweater doubles as a dressy warm-weather top and an evening sweater. The yarn is soft and drapes beautifully, so if you wish to substitute another yarn, look for a silk blend or, for a more casual top, choose a very soft cotton. This design knits up best in a low-contrast colorway, a heather, or a solid-color yarn.

SIZE DETAILS

To Fit Bust Size: 34 (38, 42, 46, 50)"
Finished Bust: 36½ (40 1/2, 44½, 48½, 52½)"
Finished Length: 20½ (21, 21½, 22, 22½)"

MATERIALS

2 (2, 3, 3, 3) skeins of Hawaii from Interlacements (80% rayon, 20% silk; 550 yds/8 oz skein) in color 103 Submarine 〈③〉

1 pair of US size 4 (3.5 mm) needles or size to obtain gauge

1 size 6 (3.5 mm), 16" circular needle

Stitch markers

GAUGE

5 sts = 1"; 8 rows = 1" in St st

PATTERNS

See charts A and B on page 81 or follow the written directions below.

Pattern A
(10-st rep plus 1 st, 28-row rep)

Row 1 (RS): Ssk, *ssk, (YO, K1) 3 times, YO, K2tog, sl 1, K2tog, psso**; rep from * to ** 8 (9, 10, 11, 12) times; ssk, (YO, K1) 3 times, YO, (K2tog) twice.

Row 2 and all even rows: Purl.

Row 3: Ssk, *K3, YO, K1, YO, K3, sl 1, K2tog, psso**; rep from * to ** 8 (9, 10, 11, 12) times; K3, YO, K1, YO, K3, K2tog.

Row 5: Ssk, *K2, YO, K3, YO, K2, sl 1, K2tog, psso**; rep from * to ** 8 (9, 10, 11, 12) times; K2, YO, K3, YO, K2, K2tog.

Row 7: Ssk, *K1, YO, K5, YO, K1, sl 1, K2tog, psso**; rep from * to ** 8 (9, 10, 11, 12) times; K1, YO, K5, YO, K1, K2tog.

Row 9: Ssk, *YO, K1, YO, ssk, K1, K2tog, YO, K1, YO, sl 1, K2tog, psso**; rep from * to ** 8 (9, 10, 11, 12) times; YO, K1, YO, ssk, K1, K2tog, YO, K1, YO, K2tog.

Row 11: Ssk, *YO, K2, YO, sl 1, K2tog, psso, YO, K2, YO, sl 1, K2tog, psso**; rep from * to ** 8 (9, 10, 11, 12) times; YO, K2, YO, sl 1, K2tog, psso, YO, K2, YO, K2tog.

Row 13: K1, (YO, K3, sl 1, K2tog, psso, K3, YO, K1) 9 (10, 11, 12, 13) times.

Row 15: K1, (YO, K1, YO, K2tog, sl 1, K2tog, psso, ssk, YO, K1, YO, K1) 9 (10, 11, 12, 13) times.

Row 17: K1, (YO, K3, sl 1, K2tog, psso, K3, YO, K1) 9 (10, 11, 12, 13) times.

Row 19: K1, (K1, YO, K2, sl 1, K2tog, psso, K2, YO, K2) 9 (10, 11, 12, 13) times.

Row 21: K1, (K2, YO, K1, sl 1, K2tog, psso, K1, YO, K3) 9 (10, 11, 12, 13) times.

Row 23: K1, (K2tog, YO, K1, YO, sl 1, K2tog, psso, YO, K1, YO, ssk, K1) 9 (10, 11, 12, 13) times.

Row 25: K1, (YO, K3, sl 1, K2tog, psso, K3, YO, K1) 9 (10, 11, 12, 13) times.

Row 27: Ssk, *K3, YO, K1, YO, K3, sl 1, K2tog, psso**; rep from * to ** 8 (9, 10, 11, 12) times; K3, YO, K1, YO, K3, K2tog.

Row 28: Purl.

Pattern B

(10-st, 28-row rep)

Row 1 (RS): *Ssk, (YO, K1) 3 times, YO, K2tog, sl 1, K2tog, psso; rep from * to end.

Row 2 and all even rows: Purl.

Row 3: *K3, YO, K1, YO, K3, sl 1, K2tog, psso; rep from * to end.

Row 5: *K2, YO, K3, YO, K2, sl 1, K2tog, psso; rep from * to end.

Row 7: *K1, YO, K5, YO, K1, sl 1, K2tog, psso; rep from * to end.

Row 9: *YO, K1, YO, ssk, K1, K2tog, YO, K1, YO, sl 1, K2tog, psso; rep from * to end.

Row 11: *YO, K2, YO, sl 1, K2tog, psso, YO, K2, YO, sl 1, K2tog, psso; rep from * to end.

Row 13: *YO, K3, sl 1, K2tog, psso, K3, YO, K1; rep from * to end.

Row 15: *YO, K1, YO, K2tog, sl 1, K2tog, psso, ssk, YO, K1, YO, K1; rep from * to end.

Row 17: *YO, K3, sl 1, K2tog, psso, K3, YO, K1; rep from * to end.

Row 19: *K1, YO, K2, sl 1, K2tog, psso, K2, YO, K2; rep from * to end.

Row 21: *K2, YO, K1, sl 1, K2tog, psso, K1, YO, K3; rep from * to end.

Row 23: *K2tog, YO, K1, YO, sl 1, K2tog, psso, YO, K1, YO, ssk, K1; rep from * to end.

Row 25: *YO, K3, sl 1, K2tog, psso, K3, YO, K1; rep from * to end.

Row 27: *K3, YO, K1, YO, K3, sl 1, K2tog, psso; rep from * to end.

Row 28: Purl.

BACK

- With straight needles, CO 91 (101, 111, 121, 131) sts. Knit 2 rows.

- On next RS row, beg patt A as shown on chart (page 81) or described above. From chart, work 1 beg st, 8 (9, 10, 11, 12) 10-st horizontal reps, and 10 end sts. Place markers between patt reps.

- Work rows 1–28 of patt once, then work rows 1–10 once more.

- Knit 2 rows.

- On next RS row, beg St st. Work even in St st until piece measures 12½".

- Beg with next RS row, work first and last 10 sts of each row in garter st, keeping body sts in St st. Rep for 8 rows total.

- When piece measures 13½", BO 5 sts at beg of next 2 rows while maintaining 5 garter sts at each edge and body in St st.

- Cont in patt until armhole measures 6½ (7, 7½, 8, 8½)".

- On next RS row, work 15 (20, 25, 30, 35) sts; attach 2nd ball of yarn and BO 49 sts for all sizes; work rem 15 (20, 25, 30, 35) sts in est patt. When armhole measures 7 (7½, 8, 8½, 9)", BO shoulder sts.

FRONT

- Work same as for back until armhole measures 3 (3½, 4, 4½, 5)". On next RS row, work 20 (25, 30, 35, 40) sts; attach 2nd ball of yarn and BO 39 sts for all sizes; work rem 20 (25, 30, 35, 40) sts in est patt.

- On next and following RS rows, dec 1 st at each neck edge 5 times. When armhole measures 7 (7½, 8, 8½, 9)", BO shoulder sts.

FINISHING

- Sew shoulder seams.

- **Neck:** With circular needle, PU 90 sts evenly spaced around neck opening, beg at left shoulder. Work in St st for 10 rnds (knit all sts), then purl 1 rnd. Turn collar inside out to reverse the RS and WS, and work 9 horizontal reps from chart B.

- Work rows 1–28 of chart, then purl 1 rnd and BO all sts loosely kw.

- Sew side seams.

- **Blocking:** Soak overnight in cold water. Roll in towel to remove excess moisture. Lay out on flat surface and, stretching lace areas slightly, pin to given dimensions. When dry, remove pins. Knead fabric very gently in hands to soften.

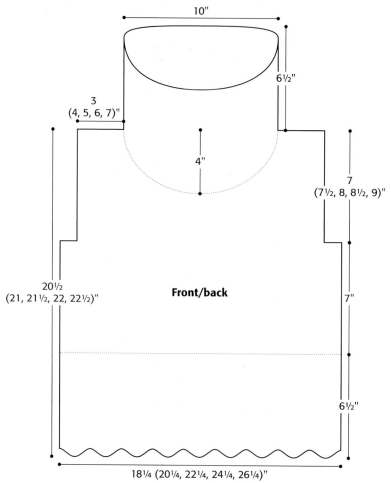

10"

6½"

3
(4, 5, 6, 7)"

4"

7
(7½, 8, 8½, 9)"

Front/back

20½
(21, 21½, 22, 22½)"

7"

6½"

18¼ (20¼, 22¼, 24¼, 26¼)"

Blue Hawaii chart A
10-st + 1 and 28-row rep

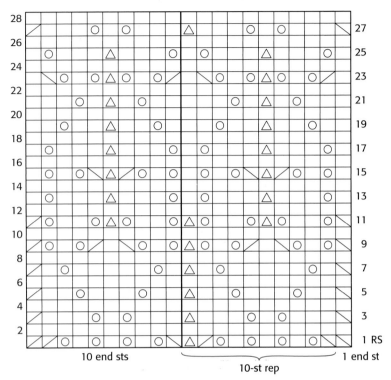

10 end sts

10-st rep

1 end st

Blue Hawaii chart B
10-st and 28-row rep

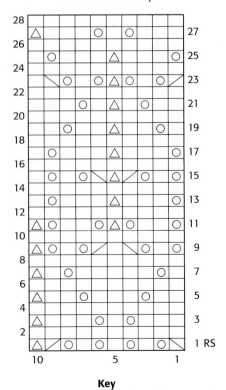

Key

☐ (RS) K1 (WS) P1	◯ YO	◸ ssk	◹ K2tog	△ Sl 1, K2tog, psso

Starburst

Starburst is another double-duty garment. It can be worn over a blouse or turtleneck as a fancy vest or alone as an evening sweater. And, it's an entry-level knitting project that could be someone's first sweater! It's knit in basic stockinette stitch with easy ribbing at bottom, neck, and armholes—what could be more beautiful or more rewarding for a beginning knitter?

When knitting with a gorgeous, colorful, fluffy yarn like this, it's best to let the yarn make the statement and to keep the details simple. The fingering-weight angora is a dream to work with, and with the uncomplicated shaping, this sweater is beautiful on any size woman.

SIZE DETAILS

To Fit Bust Size: 30 (34, 38, 42, 45)"
Finished Bust: 32½ (36, 40, 43½, 47)"
Finished Length: 20 (20, 21, 21, 22)"

MATERIALS

6 (8, 10, 12, 14) balls of Angora Super
    from Anny Blatt (70% angora,
    30% wool; 116 yds/25 g ball) in
    color Eclipse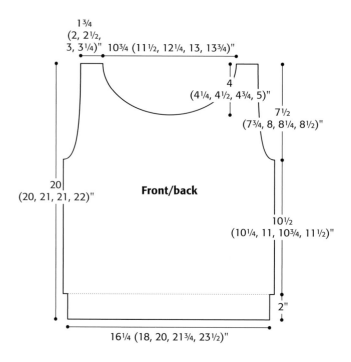

1 pair of US size 3 (3.25 mm) needles or
    size to obtain gauge

1 size 3 (3.25 mm), 16" circular needle

GAUGE

5½ sts = 1"; 8 rows = 1"

BACK AND FRONT *(Make 2)*

- With straight needles, CO 80 (90, 100, 110, 120) sts. Work K2, P2 rib for 2".

- On last WS row, inc 10 sts evenly spaced across for all sizes: 90 (100, 110, 120, 130) sts total.

- Work in St st until piece measures 12½ (12¼, 13, 12¾, 13½)", ending on a WS row.

- At beg of next 2 rows, BO 2 (3, 4, 5, 6) sts. Then on next RS and following RS rows, dec 1 st at each armhole edge 3 times for all sizes: 80 (88, 96, 104, 112) sts rem.

- Work even until armhole measures 3½" for all sizes. On next RS row, work 20 (22, 24, 26, 28) sts; attach 2nd ball of yarn and BO 40 (44, 48, 52, 56) sts; work rem 20 (22, 24, 26, 28) sts.

- On next 2 rows, BO 5 sts at each neck edge, then on next and following RS rows, dec 1 st at each neck edge 5 times: 10 (12, 14, 16, 18) sts rem per shoulder. When armhole measures 7½ (7¾, 8, 8¼, 8½)", BO shoulder sts.

FINISHING

- Sew shoulder and side seams.

- **Neck:** Using circular needle, start at left shoulder and PU 1 of every 2 sts on diagonals and 3 of every 4 sts on front and back neck BOs. Work K2, P2 rib for 1". If you need to adjust number of sts so that you'll have multiple of 4 sts to make rib patt work out, do so on left shoulder. BO loosely in rib.

- **Armholes:** Using circular needle, PU 3 of every 4 sts around armhole, beg at underarm seam. If you need to adjust number of sts, do so at underarm. Work K2, P2 rib for 1". BO loosely in rib.

- No blocking is required. Don't wash this sweater; dry-clean only.

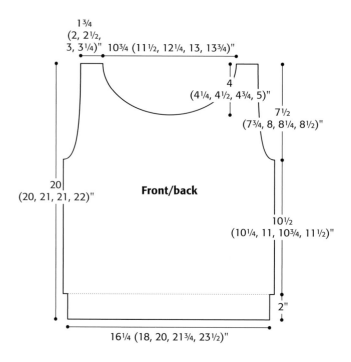

Front/back

1¾ (2, 2½, 3, 3¼)"   10¾ (11½, 12¼, 13, 13¾)"

4 (4¼, 4½, 4¾, 5)"

7½ (7¾, 8, 8¼, 8½)"

20 (20, 21, 21, 22)"

10½ (10¼, 11, 10¾, 11½)"

2"

16¼ (18, 20, 21¾, 23½)"

Watercolors

This casual, colorful, comfortable sweater is destined to become a true favorite. It's perfect for everyday wear, to toss on over a turtleneck and skirt, or to wear with a pair of well-loved jeans. Knit from a wool/cotton blend, it's a nice weight, offering warmth without being too heavy. This sweater is one you'll love wrapping up in and will want to put on first thing in the morning—even when it's old and worn and in need of a set of suede elbow patches!

SIZE DETAILS

To Fit Bust Size: 34 (38, 41, 44, 47)"
Finished Bust: 39 (43½, 46, 49¾, 53¼)"
Finished Length: 25 (25, 26, 26, 27)"
Finished Sleeve Length (from underarm): 17¼ (17¾, 18¼, 18¾, 19¼)"

MATERIALS

7 (8, 9, 10, 11) skeins of Dove from Lorna's Laces (80% wool, 20% cotton; 165 yds/2 oz skein) in color 18 Watercolor 〔3〕

1 size 7 (4.5 mm), 32" circular needle or size to obtain gauge

1 size 7 (4.5 mm), 16" circular needle

1 set of size 7 (4.5 mm) double-pointed needles

10 (10, 11, 11, 12) buttons, ⅞" or 1" diameter

Stitch markers and stitch holders

GAUGE

4½ sts = 1"; 6½ rows = 1"

BODY

- Using longer circular needle, CO 176 (196, 208, 224, 240) sts. Working back and forth, work K2, P2 rib for 2½". Switch to St st and work even until piece measures 15½ (15½, 16, 16, 16½)", ending on WS row.

- On next RS row, work 40 (45, 48, 52, 56) sts for right front, BO 8 sts for armhole, work 80 (90, 96, 104, 112) sts for back, BO 8 sts for armhole, and work rem 40 (45, 48, 52, 56) sts for left front. Set aside.

SLEEVES *(Make 2)*

- With dpns, CO 40 (40, 46, 46, 52) sts. PM for beg of rnd and join.

- Working in the round, work K2, P2 rib for 2½". On last rnd, inc 4 sts evenly spaced: 44 (44, 50, 50, 56) sts total.

- On next round, switch to St st (knit all rnds). When you have too many sts to hold on the dpns, change to the shorter circular needle. AT SAME TIME, on 9th and every subsequent 8th rnd, inc 1 st at each side of marker 9 times for all sizes.

- Work even until sleeve measures 17¼ (17¾, 18¼, 18 ¾, 19¼)". AT SAME TIME, on next to last rnd, work until 4 sts from marker, BO next 8 sts, and finish rnd. Place sts on holder and set aside.

JOINING BODY AND SLEEVES

From this point on, you will be working back and forth, not in the round.

- Working on the sweater body, K40 (45, 48, 52, 56) sts from right front; PM; K54 (54, 60, 60, 66) sleeve sts; PM; K80 (90, 96, 104, 112) sts from back; PM; K54 (54, 60, 60, 66) sleeve sts; PM; K40 (45, 48, 52, 56) sts from left front. Total sts: 268 (288, 312, 328, 356).

- Turn work and purl 1 row.

- On next RS row, knit to within 2 sts of marker, ssk, sl marker, K2tog, work across sleeve and rep dec. Work across back and rep dec. Work across sleeve sts and rep dec. Work to end of row. Total dec of 8 sts.

- On subsequent 4th rows (RS), rep dec as described 3 more times. Then work dec every RS row 21 (21, 24, 24, 27) times.

- AT SAME TIME, on front edges, when armhole depth measures 7 (7, 7½, 7½, 8)", BO 5 sts at beg of next 2 rows. Then BO 3 sts at

beg of next 2 rows. Then BO 2 sts at beg of next 4 rows. On next RS and subsequent RS row, dec 1 st at each neck edge twice.

- Work even until armhole depth measures 9½ (9½, 10, 10, 10½)". and sleeve dec are complete. BO all sts.

Finishing

- **Collar:** With shorter circular needle, PU 2 of every 3 sts on front neck BO, 1 of every 2 sts on diagonals, and 3 of every 4 sts on back neck BO. Work K2, P2 rib for 3½". (If you need to adjust the number of sts for the rib patt to work out, do so at left shoulder.) BO loosely kw.

- **Left front band:** PU 3 of every 4 sts along front edge to neck opening and work in K2, P2 rib for 1". BO loosely.

- **Right front band:** PU 3 of every 4 sts along front edge to neck opening and work 2 rows of K2, P2 rib. Mark buttonhole placement so that buttonholes are evenly spaced, approx 3" apart, with first and last buttonholes ½" from top and bottom edges (see page 11 for buttonhole schematic). Form buttonholes on next 2 rows, working each over 4 sts as follows:

  Row 1 (RS): K2tog, YO, YO, K2tog.
  Row 2 (WS): P1, P1, K1, P1.

On next RS row, resume rib patt. Work 1 more row of rib and BO all sts loosely.

- Sew underarm seams. Weave in ends.

- Sew buttons to left front band, aligning them with buttonholes on right front band. Fold back tips of collar and anchor them with buttons to sweater fronts.

- No blocking is necessary.

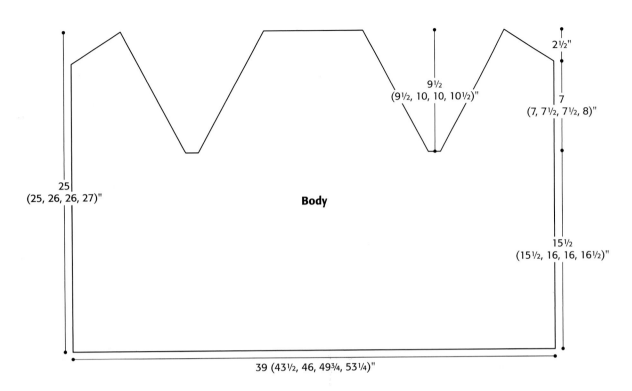

2½"

9½
(9½, 10, 10, 10½)"

7
(7, 7½, 7½, 8)"

Body

25
(25, 26, 26, 27)"

15½
(15½, 16, 16, 16½)"

39 (43½, 46, 49¾, 53¼)"

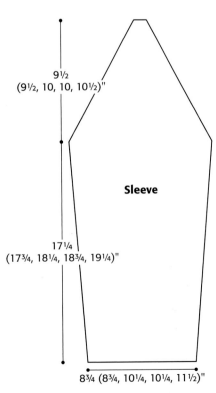

9½
(9½, 10, 10, 10½)"

Sleeve

17¼
(17¾, 18¼, 18¾, 19¼)"

8¾ (8¾, 10¼, 10¼, 11½)"

Resources

ANNY BLATT
7796 Boardwalk
Brighton, MI 48116
248-486-6160
www.annyblatt.com

DALE OF NORWAY
N16 W23390 Stoneridge Dr., Ste. A
Waukesha, WI 53188
800-441-3253
www.dale.no

INTERLACEMENTS
PO Box 3082
Colorado Springs, CO 80934
719-578-8009
www.interlacementsyarns.com

LORNA'S LACES YARNS
4229 North Honore St.
Chicago, IL 60613
773-935-3803
www.lornaslaces.com

PLASSARD YARNS
105 Dixon Drive
Chestertown, MD 21620
866-341-9425
www.plassardyarnsusa.com

PLYMOUTH YARN COMPANY
PO Box 28
Bristol, PA 19007
215-788-0459
www.plymouthyarn.com

SKASKA DESIGNS
924 W. Oak St.
Fort Collins, CO 80521
970-224-5117
www.skaska.com

UNICORN BOOKS AND CRAFTS INC.
1338 Ross St.
Petaluma, CA 94954
707-762-3362
www.unicornbooks.com

Abbreviations

approx	approximately
beg	begin(ning)
BO	bind off
CC	contrasting color
CO	cast on
cont	continue
dec	decrease(s), decreasing
dpn(s)	double-pointed needle(s)
est	established
g	grams
inc	increase(s), increasing
K	knit
K2tog	knit 2 stitches together
kw	knitwise
m	meters
MC	main color
P	purl
patt	pattern(s)
PM	place marker
psso	pass slipped stitch over
PU	pick up and knit
pw	purlwise
rem	remain(ing)
rep(s)	repeat(s)
rnd(s)	round(s)
RS	right side
sl	slip
ssk	slip, slip, knit (slip stitch as if to knit, repeat, then knit these 2 stitches together through the back)
st(s)	stitch(es)
St st	stockinette stitch
WS	wrong side
yds	yards
YO	yarn over